£1.75

85p

'MULTI-FAITH WORSHIP?'

Questions and Suggestions from the Inter-Faith Consultative Group

CHURCH HOUSE PUBLISHING
Church House, Great Smith Street, London SW1P 3NZ

ISBN 0 7151 5530 X

Published 1992 for the General Synod Board of Mission
by Church House Publishing

© *The Central Board of Finance of the Church of England 1992*

Printed in England by Rapier Press Ltd

CONTENTS

THE INTER-FAITH CONSULTATIVE GROUP
(1990-1991)

Chairman	The Rt Revd the Bishop of Wolverhampton
Members	The Revd Dr Peter Forster
	The Revd Dr Christopher Lamb
	The Rt Revd Michael Nazir-Ali
	The Revd Alan Race
	The Revd Canon Michael Wolfe
	The Revd Canon Roger Hooker (Consultant)
Representatives	Mr Alan Brown (B of ED)
	The Revd Dr Ian Kenway (BSR)
	The Revd Dr Brian Russell (ABM)
	The Revd Peter Speck (HCC)
	Dr Elaine Sugden (PWM)
	Dr Owen Cole (Archbishops' Consultants)
	The Revd Dr Clinton Bennett
Secretary	Mr Colin Podmore

The Group is grateful to the Revd Canon Dr Raymond Hammer and the Revd Jane Sinclair (a member of the Liturgical Commission) for serving on the drafting group which undertook detailed work on the booklet.

PREFACE

1   The Board of Mission notes that a growing number of services described as 'multi-faith' are taking place involving the Church of England, many of them receiving much more prominence and public attention than was the case in previous decades. Some people have called for official guidelines, but the Board does not believe that the time is yet right for this. It is not clear that the wide consensus on which guidelines issued by the House of Bishops would need to be based yet exists. Diocesan bishops may, of course, feel able to issue guidelines for their own dioceses.

2   'Multi-faith services' have taken place for decades, but for many people the whole idea is still very new and strange. There are Anglicans who oppose the concept of 'multi-faith worship' (although perhaps on reflection few would rule out everything described in this booklet under that name).[1] Others promote 'multi-faith worship' enthusiastically (although again on reflection few would accept everything described in this booklet under that name). Most members of the Church of England will find themselves somewhere between these two positions. All should recognise that no-one intends to deny Christ or act contrary to Christian doctrine.

3   Some material for a discussion of how far it is right for Christians to engage in 'multi-faith worship' already exists. The subject has been examined in several publications (including 'official' reports) over the last quarter century.[2] The Board acknowledges the value of this theological work and recognises that theological exploration will continue.

4   While such discussion proceeds, however, the Board recognises that a sizeable number of members of the Church of England believe that at least some forms of 'multi-faith' service are proper, valuable and lawful.[3] This being so, it wishes to set before those planning such services or visits to places of worship of other faiths a consideration of the issues involved and the questions posed. The Inter-Faith Consultative Group has been working on this subject for a number of

---

[1]   For a note on the use of terms such as 'multi-faith worship' see Chapter I, paras 3-5.
[2]   See Chapter II.
[3]   For the legal position, see Chapter IX.

years, and in December 1988 it was asked by the former Board for Mission and Unity to prepare the present booklet.

5   In addition to the basic theological issues which confront all Christians, 'multi-faith worship' also raises issues peculiar to the Church of England. Due to the particular place of the Church of England in our culture, its churches and ministers frequently act as focal points for the wider community, for many Christians of different traditions, and for many people of other faiths as well. In England, Anglican churches often have a greater capacity than any other religious building (or any building at all) in the area. The liturgical expression of worship and especially the Eucharist have a particular importance in the Church of England. Also, services and other events held in its churches are subject to Ecclesiastical Law. For these reasons the Board believes that there is a need for a booklet setting out the issues which arise when members of the Church of England propose to 'worship with' people of other faiths. It hopes nevertheless that much of this booklet will also be of use to other Churches and Christians.

6   The Board wishes to stress that the booklet has been prepared for use in England. It has not been possible to address the very different situations which obtain in other countries, even though members of the Group have some awareness of them. Nevertheless, it is possible that Christians from other parts of the British Isles and overseas may find it useful.

7   It was felt desirable to include a theological chapter, building on the Inter-Faith Consultative Group's earlier report, *Towards a Theology for Inter-Faith Dialogue*, which is still available. The issues which are posed by particular situations need to be considered within the context of the theology underlying our relationships in general with people of other faiths and our theological understanding of what worship is. The chapter is a further contribution to a continuing debate, and is not intended to stand on its own. This is not a doctrinal report, however. The booklet is practically focused, and the Board recommends that those who plan multi-faith activities should also consult the key theological reports and publications listed in the Bibliography. The Board hopes that, in addition to its practical value for those engaging in 'multi-faith worship', this booklet will make some contribution towards the development of a common mind on this subject both within the Church of England and in the wider Church.

8   The booklet is about 'multi-faith worship' in general. There are also specific contexts for 'multi-faith worship' which it does not address in detail. Particular issues are raised by marriages involving people of other faiths, and funerals may also require special examination.[4] Institutions such as hospitals, prisons and schools are distinctive environments. The different factors involved in each case mean that it would not be sensible to attempt to cover these highly specific contexts in this booklet. In particular, the Board would not wish the booklet to be read with school worship in mind. Worship in schools is a specialised subject which the Inter-Faith Consultative Group does not have sufficient expertise to address.

9   The Board is grateful to the Inter-Faith Consultative Group for preparing the booklet, which it believes will be a valuable resource for the continuing discussion. At various points the Group offers suggestions for consideration, but in publishing the booklet the Board does not wish to prejudge discussion in the Church as a whole by identifying itself with one set of conclusions or another to the questions the booklet poses.

17th October 1991

+ KEITH LICHFIELD
Chairman of the Board of Mission

---

[4] The Inter-Faith Consultative Group submitted a report on *The Marriage of Adherents of other Faiths in Anglican Churches* to the House of Bishops in 1989. A booklet based on this report is likely to be published in 1992.

I SITUATIONS AND QUESTIONS

1   This document arises out of the real situations and questions which Christians are already facing in many parts of Britain. By looking at some characteristic events we can see the complexities involved in arranging appropriate acts of worship. Here are some examples:

a.   The local or regional Scouts are planning for the annual St George's Day service, and come to the minister asking that the service should include some acknowledgement of the presence of 'Indian boys' in the movement. On inquiry it turns out that all these boys are Hindu and Sikh, and the Scout leaders assume that some 'prayers from their books' may be appropriate.
Should such prayers be included? If so, how are the Indian boys likely to feel? If they are included, how are they to be selected? Who should read them, and in what language?

b.   A children's charity wants to celebrate its jubilee with a service in the cathedral, and in discussion with the precentor its officials point out that the number of Asian families among its clients is steadily growing. Again the 'Asian families' concerned are Muslim, Sikh and Hindu.
Is it possible to involve some representatives of the Asian families in the service? Since they represent at least three different religious traditions can any significant elements from their faiths be included without unbalancing the service?

c.   The new mayor is a Sikh, but has asked for a Christian chaplain and a civic service in the parish church to mark his year of office. Nevertheless it is clear that he would be glad if some affirming reference to his own faith could be included in the worship. He suggests a reading from the Guru Granth Sahib.
Is this request acceptable? What will it mean as part of a Christian service? If it is refused what impression is being given about the place of Sikhs in civic life and of Christian tolerance? If the next mayor asks for a service in the mosque or synagogue of which she or he is a member, how should Christian councillors respond?

d.   It is being suggested by some in the city that the annual Remembrance Day service in the Cathedral should include participation by representatives of the Hindu, Muslim, Sikh and Jewish communities whose members also lost their lives in the wars of this century. The city's Muslim community is quite large and the leading imam would be prepared to give a short address, as the Methodist and Roman Catholic leaders have done in different years.

Would this be acceptable? If the imam is invited to speak who will represent the smaller numbers of Hindus and Sikhs and the tiny Jewish community?

e.   Disaster has struck in the area, and the death-toll includes people of many faiths. The clergy are expected to reflect this fact in the memorial service for the victims which will take place in the local park. Civic dignitaries expect that the leaders of other faiths will be asked to take part.

How can this be made an occasion which expresses the grief of the whole local community including those nurtured outside the Christian tradition?

f.   A new, vigorous local group is concerned with environmental and ecological issues, and has been well supported by Hindu and Buddhist members. The group has written to the Cathedral to say that they want to launch an appeal for members and funds, and to begin with a big multi-faith event in the cathedral.

Can an event be devised which is faithful to Christian insights about green issues, and also draws upon other religious traditions? Will it make any difference if it is called a 'celebration' rather than a 'service'?

g.   The local interfaith group is holding its big annual function in the Town Hall. This always includes a time of prayer led by people of different religious traditions. This year is their tenth anniversary and they have asked the Bishop to preside and lead the prayers.

What should he do, knowing that several Christians have expressed great unease about this occasion in the past?

h.   The Sikhs have opened a community welfare centre next to their gurdwara, with the encouragement of some local clergy. Wanting to build on this link, they decide to invite the Bishop to visit the gurdwara at *Baisakhi*, the next major festival. This is the first time the Sikhs have issued such an invitation to a local church leader.

How can the Bishop discover what will be expected of him in the temple? He will have to cover his head and remove his shoes, but will he acknowledge the presence of the Sikh scriptures with a reverent bow, and if so, will he be endorsing their validity?

2   It is not possible to offer ready-made responses to each and every situation that can arise in a local community in England where different faith communities are considering possible worship together. But some principles and suggestions can be proposed that may enable people to develop good practice. However, before reviewing the recent history of multi-faith worship in England and introducing some theological perspectives, it is important to face the problem of definition.

The Term 'Multi-Faith Worship'

3   The term 'multi-faith worship' can be used to cover a wide range of events. These include, at one end, services of one faith at which people of other faiths may be present in the congregation, and, at the other, events in which elements from a variety of religions are blended together. These are not stark alternatives. Between them lies a range of types of event, and different people will find the limit of what they can accept at different points.

4   The very term 'multi-faith worship' is the subject of debate. For a long time the description 'interfaith worship' was the most common. Some wish to avoid using the word 'worship', preferring another term such as 'service', 'observance', 'celebration', 'ceremony', 'event', 'act of witness' or 'meditation'. Similarly, 'all faiths', 'multifaith', 'interfaith' and 'faith to faith' each have their supporters. The inverted commas in the title reflect this discussion. But words have differing meanings for different people and at different times. A description preferred by some, now, because they invest it with a particular meaning (or lack of a particular meaning) may have no meaning at all, or a different (possibly less acceptable) meaning to others, or in the future.

5   Each of the terms available poses problems, but the phenomenon in question has to be called something! The Group has chosen to use the term 'multi-faith worship' (except when quoting from documents which use other terms) because it regards 'multi-faith worship' as a comparatively neutral term.

II NOT A NEW QUESTION

6 Awareness of 'multi-faith worship' in England grew in the late 1980s following a series of events in Anglican cathedrals, but 'multi-faith worship' in Britain is by no means new. One of the first large public services involving people of other faiths was the memorial service for Sir Francis Younghusband, founder of the World Congress of Faiths, in 1942. The World Congress of Faiths later organised other services, including one marking the Coronation in 1953 and an annual All Faiths Service.

7 However, it was in the mid-1960s that such services gained prominence and became more frequent. In 1965 the Duke of Edinburgh attended a multi-faith 'Ceremony of Religious Affirmation' at St Mary-le-Bow to mark the opening of the Commonwealth Arts Festival. In 1966 the Queen attended a similar service for Commonwealth Day at St Martin-in-the-Fields. This has grown into the Observance for Commonwealth Day which she now attends each year in Westminster Abbey.

Statement on Inter-Faith Services (BCC, 1968)

8 In the autumn of 1966 a sparsely-attended meeting of the Lower House of the Convocation of Canterbury resolved 'that this house views with concern the holding of multi-religious services in Christian churches'. In April 1967 the General Secretaries of the larger missionary societies and Canon David Paton, Secretary of the Missionary and Ecumenical Council of the Church Assembly (MECCA), issued a statement which concluded:

> while true dialogue between Christians and adherents of other religions is to be encouraged, local churches should be strongly advised not to provide for inter-faith services.

9 That autumn, Canon Paton asked the Assembly of the British Council of Churches to endorse this statement, but instead it commissioned a report. The resulting *Statement on Inter-Faith Services* advocated the exploration of

(a) exchanges of visits for sympathetic and instructed observation of one another's worship; and

(b) occasions on which those of different faiths do in turn what is characteristic of their own religion, enabling the others present to share to the extent to which they conscientiously can. (p.4)

10 The 1968 Spring Assembly received this report 'with appreciation' and passed a resolution encouraging member churches and councils of churches to help their members

(a) to engage in common action with their neighbours of other faiths and to seek ways of affirming with them our common humanity and yearning for justice, brotherhood and peace;

(b) to arrange with due care occasions on which those of different faiths may engage in informed dialogue and give unambiguous testimony to their beliefs;

(c) to take opportunity where permitted for sympathetic observation of the worship of other faiths and so make possible a deeper understanding;

(d) to accept gladly whatever experience of communion with God arises in such relationships.

The resolution concluded:

In pursuing these aims, Churches should scrupulously avoid those forms of inter-faith worship which compromise the distinctive faiths of the participants and should ensure that Christian witness is neither distorted nor muted.

The BCC report was studied and approved by MECCA's annual consultation in 1969.

Inter-faith Worship (World Congress of Faiths, 1974)

11 In the late 1960s and early 1970s the number and variety of 'multi-faith services' increased. They were organised by Community Relations Councils, branches of the United Nations Association and organisations such as the Girl Guide Movement and the YWCA. This increase, together with an awareness of widespread criticisms of such occasions, prompted the then Archdeacon Edward Carpenter, as President of the World Congress of Faiths (which had been a pioneer of 'multi-faith worship' in Britain), to convene an ecumenical group of Christian clergy to examine the theological issues. Its report, *Inter-faith*

Worship (published in 1974), was edited by the group's secretary, the Revd Marcus Braybrooke.

12   The group's members were 'all sympathetic to the aims and ideals of the World Congress of Faiths', but 'tried to understand why some Christians conscientiously oppose any form of inter-faith worship'. The group hoped that its study would 'remove some misunderstandings and lead to an increased appreciation of the value of such occasions'. (p.2)

13   The report examined reasons commonly advanced in favour of 'multi-faith worship' and sought to answer objections. It also took account of the views of other faiths. Its Conclusion advocated the attendance of people of one religion at the worship of another, but also saw a need for 'specially designed acts of common worship', which, however, 'should not replace the normal worship of any religious tradition'. (p.13) It offered some brief guidance on the planning of services.

Inter-Faith Worship? (Grove Booklets, 1977)

14   In 1977 Grove Booklets published *Inter-Faith Worship?* by the Revd Peter Akehurst and Canon R.W.F. Wootton. They noted that Britain's 'new pluralism' led to 'pressures for common worship', which required 'new standards and guidelines for inter-faith worship'. While acknowledging the situation and the demand for 'all-faiths services', the authors entered a note of caution. The booklet sought to 'raise issues of principle which need prior consideration'. The authors pleaded 'that we relate to the theology of worship and mission as well as to the practicalities and expediencies of this new situation'. (p.5)

15   After an examination of worship, the authors asked whether people of different faiths 'are doing intrinsically the same thing when they worship, or whether it is a case of separate and different things being done side by side'. They believed that the distinctiveness of worship in different religions was such that 'it cannot easily be engaged in together and that if this is to be attempted very clear guidelines and safeguards need to be set out'. Some examples of 'multi-faith worship', 'which appear almost to be a conscious attempt to blur theological exactitude', were to be deplored. (pp.9f)

16   The authors pleaded for:

> a deliberately low profile worship, not a debased coin – for worship based in a creaturely, behavioural stance, exploring techniques of worship together, affirming values together, and engaging in the silence of listening and meditation together. . . It could validly be done in the context of modern pluralistic society. If it is theologically too threatening and unsatisfying to piece together a mosaic of bits from the classic sacred texts of the world's faiths and liturgies, less pretence may be involved in setting limited aims of this nature. (p.10)

17   The booklet went on to consider 'the missionary dimension' and 'the practical dimension', including the use of church buildings by people of other faiths and 'visiting other worshipping groups'. It reviewed examples of 'avowed multi-faith worship'. In conclusion, the authors offered five guidelines:

1. It is best to set limited aims.
2. They must be based on mutual respect.
3. They should grow out of prior relationship.
4. They must avoid theological inconsistency.
5. They must avoid situational dishonesty.

They commented, 'We believe worship within these guidelines would be for the glory of God and the service of man.' (p.22)

Inter-faith Services and Worship
(Archbishops' Consultants on Interfaith Relations, 1979)

18   In 1979 a working group of the Archbishops' Consultants on Interfaith Relations produced a report on *Interfaith Services and Worship* (published in *Ends and Odds* in 1980).

19   The report believed that

> Given this context ('the interfaith situation in Britain today') interfaith services are not contrived or artificial. Indeed, they are likely to increase. However, there are a host of other factors, such as the temptation to stunts, popular syncretism, exploitation by fringe groups, and fascination with the occult, that could all too easily lead to a misuse of interfaith services.

20   It distinguished between the types of service, described for convenience as:

A.   Christian services with guest participants from other faiths.
B.   Interfaith services of the serial multi-faith type.
C.   Interfaith services with an agreed common order of service.

The report regarded all three types as acceptable, and offered comments and suggestions on each in turn, concluding with advice on attending the worship of other faiths.[5]

21   The report saw multi-faith services as 'occasional additions to the regular liturgical life of the Christian Church and not a substitute for it'.

> Interfaith is not a new religion. The meeting which we welcome is of committed members of the Household of Faith. Equality is of believers and not of beliefs.

The report concluded:

> We hope that in their proper place, Interfaith Services can help to give the Church a new vision of the greatness and glory of God and can strengthen Christians in welcoming, loving and serving others in the spirit and for the sake of him who died for all mankind.

Relations with people of Other Faiths: Guidelines for Dialogue in Britain (Committee for Relations with People of Other Faiths, BCC, 1981/3)

22   The Committee for Relations with People of Other Faiths, established in June 1978, published its *Guidelines for Dialogue in Britain* three years later. These included a brief section on multi-faith services and the use of church property, which commented:

> Discovering what seem to be common spiritual experiences among people of different faiths, some Christians have gone ahead and attempted worship together or have participated in joint acts of witness. Other Christians with equally genuine convictions refuse to take such a step. Certainly such ventures are fraught with difficulty and ambiguity. What is agreed is that rushing into inter-faith worship out of vague feelings of cordiality or denouncing it without examination as apostasy, are alike reprehensible. (p.19)

---

[5] For elucidation of these types of service, see Chapters V, VII and VIII below.

15

Can We Pray Together? Guidelines on Worship in a Multi-Faith Society (Committee for Relations with People of Other Faiths, BCC, 1983)

23   In 1983 the Committee published a thirty-page sequel to its *Guidelines*, in an attempt 'to explore what can happen when people of different faiths meet one another in the context of worship or prayer'. Its hope was to 'give constructive guidance both to those who want to explore the ways of prayer together with people of other faiths and to those who have genuine misgivings about such ventures'. (Foreword)

24   After examining the context in which the question arises, and 'worship' in the different religions, *Can We Pray Together?* explored the relevance of dialogue to the subject of worship together and offered four Bible studies. The history of 'multi-faith worship' in Britain was briefly surveyed. The booklet considered the role of silence, the attitudes of the churches and the special cases of hospitals and schools, marriages and funerals. Guidance on visiting other places of worship and 'resources for worship in a multi-faith society' were offered.

25   The central section, entitled 'Inter-Faith Services', covered the types of service and planning a service, but not in great detail. The present booklet aims to build on this previous work and offer fuller material on these subjects.[6]

---

[6]   D. Bookless, *Interfaith Worship and Christian Truth* (Grove Worship Series No. 117, 1991) was published after the text of the present booklet was completed.

16

III SOME THEOLOGICAL PERSPECTIVES

Setting the Scene

26 In July 1984 the General Synod received the report *Towards a Theology for Inter-Faith Dialogue*. This was re-published for the 1988 Lambeth Conference, with an additional essay by Bishop Michael Nazir-Ali which drew in particular upon his experience and knowledge of multi-faith relations in other parts of the Anglican Communion. Other formal responses to this earlier report were also offered, and in considering the specific question of 'multi-faith worship' we have attempted to build upon the foundations which have already been laid. This chapter cannot reproduce the detailed argument of the earlier report, to which interested readers are referred. Instead, from the conclusion of that study we trace some theological issues relating to the issue of 'multi-faith worship'.

27 As has commonly been the case in multi-faith literature, the discussion in *Towards a Theology for Inter-Faith Dialogue* was structured around three theoretical positions: exclusivism, inclusivism and pluralism. Exclusivism emphasises the uniqueness and finality of Jesus Christ, and the necessity for salvation of explicit confession of Jesus Christ. While holding firmly to the belief that God was supremely and definitively manifest in Jesus, inclusivism also seeks to affirm the power and presence of God within adherents of other religions, and indeed through the whole of creation. Different opinions are held about the special place, if any, which religious activity outside Christianity has in mediating the presence of God. Pluralism is concerned to view the differences between religions as arising from the different human interpretations of the revelation of the one God according to cultural limitations, and this may (but need not necessarily) involve a belief that all religions are on a similar level in relation to ultimate truth.

28 It is acknowledged that each category may involve a variety of standpoints, and it is possible to embrace elements of each; indeed, different writers tend to define the categories rather differently. In his recent book, *The Gospel in a Pluralist Society* (SPCK, 1989), Bishop Lesslie Newbigin summarises his own attempt to draw aspects of the three approaches together as follows:

> The position which I have outlined is exclusivist in the sense that it affirms the unique truth of the revelation in Jesus Christ, but it is not exclusivist in the sense of denying the possibility of the salvation of the non-Christian. It

17

is inclusivist in the sense that it refuses to limit the saving grace of God to the members of the Christian Church, but it rejects the inclusivism which regards the non-Christian religions as vehicles of salvation. It is pluralist in the sense of acknowledging the gracious work of God in the lives of all human beings, but it rejects a pluralism which denies the uniqueness and decisiveness of what God has done in Jesus Christ. (p.182f).

29   Bishop Newbigin's summary represents one line of response to the position outlined in *Towards a Theology for Inter-Faith Dialogue*, and relates closely to the additional essay by Bishop Michael Nazir-Ali published in the Lambeth Conference edition. These responses are concerned to emphasise that while an assertion of the activity of God through Christ outside the visible confines of the Church is entirely proper, this has to be kept in a clear relation to his activity in the incarnate Christ. While the presence and work of God may to a degree be mediated through various languages, cultures and religious traditions, what constitutes such 'salvation histories' can only be determined when there is a normative Salvation History against which other traditions might be judged. Bishop Nazir-Ali concluded his discussion of the Christology of *Towards a Theology for Inter-Faith Dialogue* as follows:

> The fact of the matter is that the Word has *become* flesh, not simply manifested itself in the flesh. Jesus Christ is the full, definitive and final revelation of God for us. Whatever else may be claimed of God, it is to be judged in the light of this definitive revelation which takes place in the full light of history, though, of course, it points to that which is beyond history. The history of the man Jesus is inescapably, finally and irrevocably tied up with the eternal Word and the one cannot be understood without the other. (p.48)

30   A rather different development of *Towards a Theology for Inter-Faith Dialogue* can be found in, for example, Kenneth Cracknell's *Towards a New Relationship* (Epworth Press, 1986), chapter 5. Mr Cracknell (who was one of the authors of the original report) emphasises the independence of the eternal *Logos* or Word of God from the historical Jesus Christ, in whom the *Logos* fully dwelt for a period. But, independently of the incarnation in the man Jesus Christ, the *Logos* is active as God's agent in revelation and providence throughout all time. Some of the early Fathers of the Church, notably St Justin Martyr and St Clement of Alexandria, are invoked in Cracknell's support. A high place is still given to the activity of the *Logos* in Jesus Christ, as the

supreme revelation of the nature of God as love, a love which extends to the cross, where God as the *Logos* truly suffers for creation. Yet the difference between the activity of God in Christ and in other human beings is cast as one of 'immeasurable degree, not of absolute kind' (p.102f).

31   These lines of response to *Towards a Theology for Inter-Faith Dialogue* could readily be multiplied, most obviously by considering positions like that of John Hick, who adopts a more radical pluralism of religious faiths. In a series of publications, Hick has pleaded for a 'Copernican revolution' which would centre all human religious response on God, or what he terms as 'the Real'. This latter expression is chosen to incorporate the non-theistic traditions from within Buddhism and Hinduism into the overall picture. (See, for example, *God Has Many Names* (Macmillan, 1980) and *An Interpretation of Religion* (Macmillan, 1989)). The revelation of God in Christ is thereby held to be of value alongside other revelations, whose moral and spiritual fruits are equally as impressive as those of Christianity. While all religions provide a context for 'salvation' or 'liberation', it remains an open and empirical question, on Hick's view, whether one tradition has achieved 'salvation' to a greater degree than any other.

32   The past two decades have produced a large volume of writing on these subjects, and the many different points of view which have been explored and argued have their supporters. In modified forms, each of the three approaches just outlined are represented among the authors of this booklet. Our attempts to achieve a consensus upon the central theological, and especially Christological, issues which arise have to a significant degree failed, and further attention to the theology of multi-faith questions will clearly be required in the coming years, even if a full consensus on such issues is never likely to be reached. Because the opposition to, or caution concerning, 'multi-faith worship' is generally strongest among those who place considerable emphasis upon the uniqueness and finality of Jesus Christ, the remainder of this chapter is written largely from that perspective. This both illustrates how such a theology need not preclude some forms, and occasions, of 'multi-faith worship', and indicates how Christian discernment in this area might proceed. This perspective should not, however, be presumed to be narrowly 'exclusivist' in the sense defined at the start of this chapter; rather, like Newbigin and Nazir-Ali, it attempts to draw from a broad range of biblical material.

The Witness of Scripture

33   A Christian's first, and unswerving loyalty should be to God as revealed and embodied in Jesus Christ. Yet, properly understood, the uniqueness of Jesus Christ as saviour of the world need not preclude, and indeed might well be seen to indicate, his universality. Throughout both Old and New Testaments we see the wider and ultimately universal significance of the particular and unique activity of God in Israel and Jesus Christ. At the same time we see a recurring failure of the witnesses of God's activity to appreciate its universal dimension. Our starting point, then, should be an open-hearted loyalty to Jesus Christ which honours both his uniqueness and his universality, and does not play one off against the other. For example, an unbalanced emphasis upon the uniqueness and finality of Jesus Christ has sometimes led to a narrow vision of God's relation to the world, and too great a separation of the Church from the world. On the other hand, unless the proper Christian claims concerning the uniqueness and finality of Jesus Christ are upheld, there might be a drift towards the syncretism which critics and opponents of 'multi-faith worship' rightly fear.

34   In connection with potential multi-faith occasions, there are three important factors which might be drawn from scripture to further guide our approach.

35   *First*, there is the challenging, even baffling, aspect of the Christian faith that we often find Christ where we least expect him, like those declared righteous in the parable of the sheep and the goats (Matthew 25), or the good Samaritan who, in the parable, is the one furthest removed from orthodox religion. If the whole world belongs to Christ, and is under his rule, we should acknowledge his potential to be present in unexpected circumstances, reflecting the pattern of Bethlehem, Golgotha, and indeed of the Bible as a whole. The Melchizedek incident (Genesis 14) and the story of Balaam (Numbers 22-24) are a recognition in the Old Testament that God not only speaks to and through those who stand outside God's chosen people, but that he uses them to speak to us, in order to enlarge our vision.

36   *Secondly*, there is the charismatic dimension of the life of the Church, which entails that we should be open to a particular moving of

God's Spirit in particular circumstances. Thus, for example, if the general rule is that acts of worship are not modified to take account of the presence of those of other faiths, it is perfectly possible to envisage exceptional or unusual circumstances leading to an exceptional liturgical provision. It is difficult to generalise in advance about such situations, which might take a myriad of forms, but we should be open to them. There will always be firm limits. For example, Christians will never want to engage in idolatry, or deny Christ.

37   At one level, the story of Naaman the Syrian (2 Kings 5) ends with Elisha permitting Naaman to continue in the cult of the Syrian god, Rimmon, in recognition of the social and cultural difficulties facing Naaman. But this permission for Naaman to be a secret believer, who could continue to observe non-Israelite religious traditions, only follows after Naaman acknowledges the need to ask pardon of Yahweh and his prophet for continuing in the worship of Rimmon. The theme of peaceful relations between Israel and Syria underlies the incident (v.7), and the principle that a certain flexibility in multi-faith relations might be adopted in order to safeguard and secure better relations between two or more cultural communities might be drawn from this story. However, the Old Testament material (in relation to Syria, for example, see Isaiah 7) which warns against any compromise deriving from a fear of the power or influence of other peoples will also have to be borne in mind when Scripture is interpreted for contemporary contexts.

38   It is interesting to note that the Old Testament does not always look for conversion in a later Christian sense on the part of those who stand outside Israel, but rather for recognition and acknowledgement of Yahweh as the true God, even while those who make the recognition remain within their own cultural and religious contexts. Not only Naaman fits this category, but also, for example, Jethro (Exodus 18), Nebuchadnezzar (Daniel 4), and the pagan sailors and people of Nineveh of the Book of Jonah. If the situation is somewhat different with the transformation of the Old Covenant into the New Covenant, with a greater emphasis in Christianity upon conversion to an explicit Christian confession, the contrast should not be overplayed, and we have much to learn from the Old Testament standpoint.

21

39. The story of Naaman the Syrian speaks of tolerance towards other worship traditions, and of the granting of permission, under certain circumstances, for a believer in Yahweh to participate in those traditions. The story of St Paul's encounter with Athenian religion (Acts 17) expresses the same point from a different perspective. In his missionary encounter with the Athenians, Paul makes a positive evaluation of the 'religiousness' of the Athenians and quotes from what may be regarded as their sacred scriptures, the Poets. He uses a quotation from these writings to assert that Christians and non-Christians alike are to be regarded as 'God's offspring'. Paul does not wish to confuse his own faith and that of the Athenians – he makes the 'unknown' known, and condemns idolatry – but neither does he wish his judgement upon the Athenian religion to be purely negative. Their religious traditions, it might be claimed, were in part a response to the calling of the unnamed, cosmic Christ, and as such were regarded by Paul as part of God's gracious preparation for the full proclamation of the Gospel. Paul's judgement did not entail a general positive evaluation of other worship traditions, so much as a spiritual discernment that the hearts of those he encountered in Athens were by no means entirely turned away from God by their religious observances.

40 *Thirdly*, there is the important principle classically enunciated by St Paul in 1 Corinthians 8-10, that individual Christians have to weigh their actions in the light of the particular Christian community of which they are a part. While in theory certain things are potentially lawful, in practice they may be disruptive to the life – and witness – of the Church. The term 'community' will have to be interpreted flexibly; in the contemporary Church of England an Anglican may have varying links with an individual parish, a group of parishes, a deanery and a diocese, not to mention ecumenical and international relationships. While it will always be inevitable, and right, that individual people and groups will seek to take innovative initiatives in the life of the Church, this has to be tempered with a proper regard to the views of the remainder of the Church. This principle has a particular application to multi-faith relations, where the specialist knowledge involved often leads to the primary involvement of a relatively small, and perhaps enthusiastic, group. It need not be inferred that problematic situations will necessarily result from the activity of those with a particular interest, and a corresponding knowledge, of multi-faith issues. Indeed, there is some evidence that problems most often arise when enthusiasts without specialist knowledge or advice launch out into 'multi-faith worship'.

41   The argument in 1 Corinthians 8-10 is carefully nuanced, and is addressed to a specific and problematic situation in the early Church. The interpretation and application of these chapters in very different contexts today will have to weigh with care Paul's underlying principles, rather than assuming a one-to-one correspondence with contemporary multi-faith issues. We have long realised that a similar process of interpretation is required in relation to Paul's instructions in that letter upon marriage and the social role of women. The underlying principles of his discussion of meat sacrificed to idols are firstly, that whatever is done must be done in love; secondly, that idols have no absolute or real existence; thirdly, that scandal and division in the Church are to be avoided; fourthly, that God is one, and worship not directed to the one God is demonic; and, fifthly, that whatever action a Christian decides upon, it should in conscience be motivated by a desire to glorify God and serve the mission of the Church, as far as possible avoiding 'giving offence to Jews or to Greeks or to the Church of God... not seeking my own advantage, but that of many, that they may be saved' (1 Corinthians 10.32f).

42   Similar practical questions arise today for Christians who are in close contact with other faith communities. What advice should be given to Christians who want to know whether it is permissible to eat the meat of sacrificial animals or other foods? This question can often arise in multi-faith contexts. Generally speaking, the advice might be to refrain, especially in a formal religious context. But there will be certain situations where, for the sake of the Gospel, a different course of action would commend itself to Christian freedom. And out of a formal religious context, for example in some social situations, provided such action would not stir controversy in the local Church, there need be no anxiety about participation. But these are general rules, which would need to be considered in the actual contexts confronting a believer, and Christians should strive to be tolerant of differing responses among themselves to such situations.

Exploring Worship

43   St Paul's argument in 1 Corinthians was influenced by his understanding of the Eucharist, and it is important to acknowledge that the sacramental character of central acts of Christian worship sets limits to occasions of 'multi-faith worship'. The rituals of Baptism and

Eucharist derive their central meaning from their re-presentation, or remembrance, of the unique historical death and resurrection of Christ. For all its properly universal range, the uniqueness of the saving history of Christ imparts a distinct character to the central Christian rituals which respond to it. Up to a point, the same may be said of non-sacramental acts of worship which include a sermon, or the public reading of Scripture. Quite severe limits are set to what we might properly attempt in the area of 'multi-faith worship', in that it cannot include the central Christian sacramental actions which recall to us the saving events of the Gospel. Inevitably there will be a tendency towards a somewhat restricted 'highest common factor' approach, if we are faithful to our Lord. Yet this is not really a discouragement, and in its own way offers us the invitation to explore what might properly be offered to God in multi-faith contexts.

44 'Multi-faith worship' will not form part of the 'normal' diet of Christian worship, and will generally arise in special circumstances; a common concern, a shared grief, a communal celebration. Christians in this country may feel that they lose much by the limitations which the situation imposes on the liturgical structure. This will be more than matched by the losses which other faith communities may face if the event is conducted in English (which may not be their mother tongue) and in unfamiliar surroundings. What is lost may in part be regained by the other dimensions which the multi-faith character adds to an occasion which has its own intrinsic vigour. The splendour of the traditional Commonwealth Day Observance well illustrates this process. In the absence of the sense of a special occasion it might be doubted whether 'multi-faith worship' would develop a wide appeal in the Church, although for some people a desire for 'multi-faith worship' will also spring from on-going relationships of encounter and dialogue. From this perspective, the desire for 'multi-faith worship' becomes part of the search for truth itself, and provides new data for a continuing theological exploration. Some would wish to give considerable emphasis to this perspective on 'multi-faith worship'.

45 Thus far we have used the term 'worship' somewhat loosely, and in the past events which might have merited the description 'multi-faith worship' have often been called 'observances', 'celebrations', and so forth. In part this has been intended to discourage controversy, although in its own way it points to the somewhat reduced character of

these events when compared with mainstream Christian worship. But too much should not be made of the particular language chosen, especially as the modern concept of worship in western Christianity has arguably become too narrowly defined in terms of specially time-tabled events in specially designated buildings. Our need to re-establish a proper relation between such worship and the offering of our everyday activity to God, between liturgy and lifestyle, suggests that we need to broaden our commonly received concept of worship.

46   There is no doubt that Christian participation in interfaith activities with elements of common worship will raise matters of concern. Above all, there must be no slide into either syncretism (a thoughtless confusion of different faith traditions) or idolatry (giving worship to that which is not God). But the existence of dangers is not in itself an argument for avoiding a responsible exploration in this area. There will be a particular need for the oversight of the Bishop.

47   All worship is exploration, and it would be a mistake to think that the current practice of mainstream Christian worship is either beyond criticism, or has an intrinsic finality about it. As the story of Jesus' encounter with the Samaritan woman (John 4) makes clear, although the Judaeo-Christian tradition of worship has a special place in God's purposes, it, together with other traditions which 'worship what they do not know', will be transcended and fulfilled in Christ. In our worship we should be aware that we experience the kingdom of God which has been established in Jesus Christ but which is not yet fully realised. The western tradition of worship has arguably concentrated too much upon the achievement of an unambiguous 'pure' worship, in order somehow to secure God's blessing upon it, and those taking part. Perhaps we need to focus more upon the *intention* of our worship, acknowledging that, precisely because it passes into the mystery of God, it will be provisional and anticipatory, pointing beyond itself. Whilst the Church on earth may join in the worship of the hosts of heaven here and now (Revelation 5.13) its worship looks forward to a greater completion. Similarly, but to deeper and varying degrees, we may regard the worship of those of other faiths as incomplete, but not necessarily wholly misplaced. This is the most natural reading of a verse such as Malachi 1.11, where Malachi claims for God worship which is not explicitly offered in his name, but is sincere and validated by a pure heart:

For from the rising of the sun to its setting, my name is great among the nations, and in every place incense is offered to my name, and a pure offering, for my name is great among the nations. (RSV)

48   Other interpretations of this verse have been offered: for example, that it refers either to Jewish proselytes, converts from among the nations, or to Jewish worship in the so-called Diaspora, where Jews were scattered among the nations, or that it expresses a dream and a hope, rather than an existing state of affairs. Many early Christian writers adopted this last interpretation in order to undergird from the Old Testament the universal aims of the Church's missionary activity, and later it was regarded as prophetic of the sacrifice of the Eucharist.[7] Furthermore, the overall context of Malachi 1 is a contrast between the condemnation of the Jewish worship of the restored Temple in Jerusalem and the surprisingly acceptable worship of the surrounding peoples. The chapter ends with the claim that God's 'name is feared among the nations', where the word for 'feared' has the positive Old Testament connotation of a due reverence. The distinguished British Baptist scholar H.H. Rowley was thus drawn to say of Malachi 1, 'Malachi claims for Jehovah worship that is not offered to his name but is sincere and validated by a pure heart' (*The Missionary Message of the Old Testament* (Oxford, 1945), p.73). This positive evaluation need not imply an unqualified approval of the Gentile 'offering', and may be emphasised in this chapter in order to point up the condemnation of current Israelite worship. The degree to which the word 'offering' refers to the cultic worship of the Gentiles, rather than to their attitude of heart and mind, has also been much debated, although some reference to non-Israelite cultic worship can hardly be denied.

49   If Malachi claims that the worship of other nations is more acceptable than the profanities currently offered at Jerusalem, it also suggests that the names of the gods addressed are in some sense identical with that of Yahweh, the Lord of hosts. If we need to be

---

[7] The NIV translation adopts this future reference, but on textual grounds this is an unlikely interpretation. The Hebrew has no verb, simply the object 'my name' and the predicate 'great'. The idiomatic omission of the verb 'to be' in Hebrew prose is used overwhelmingly for the present tense, not the future, where the verb is generally supplied.

cautious in drawing such a conclusion, the very logic of monotheism poses the question. If there is only one God who actually exists, then other gods which are either mentioned directly, or implied, in the Bible must either be made subservient to God or somehow subsumed into him. In each case, we would be drawn to conclude that amid its ambiguity and incompleteness worship directed to 'other gods', inasmuch as it is accepted by the true God, is directed to him. Of course, there is much material in the Bible which emphasises the uniqueness of Yahweh, and his exclusive claim to be worshipped, but it is precisely this radical exclusivity which leads to his ability to be present universally, even in the worship of non-Israelite religions. Other texts besides Malachi 1 make this kind of thinking possible, for example those describing Nebuchadnezzar (Daniel 4.34-37), Darius (Daniel 6.25-27) and the people of Assyria and Egypt (Isaiah 19.16-25 – although this text has a future reference) as worshipping Yahweh. Even in Deuteronomy, which contains texts which strongly deny the existence of other gods, there are hints that these 'gods' have been given to the gentile nations by the true God – see, for example, Deuteronomy 4.19; 29.26. Provided that the worship of such 'gods' was not brought into competition, or syncretistic alliance, with mainstream Israelite worship, we can see how it had a place in God's purposes and was in a real if limited sense directed to him.

50   This chapter has not attempted a full discussion of the theological issues which surround the question of 'multi-faith worship', but it has outlined how a limited but positive place for some forms of 'multi-faith worship' can be justified even from the theological viewpoints which might most suggest caution. Of course, many Christians feel able to go beyond this cautious approach. The chapter concludes with two brief sections, on the meaning of worship in other religious traditions and on the question of idols and images.

'Worship' for People of Other Faiths

51   It is difficult for Christians to come to any judgement about 'multi-faith worship' without knowing what people of other faiths think is happening in their own regular forms of worship. It is not possible to expound what this is for each separate faith tradition here. That would take many pages of detailed explanation, and it would in any case need a Hindu, a Muslim, and a Jewish (etc) scholar to comment adequately.

Some Muslims would regard only the ritual Islamic prayer of *salat* or *namaz* as real worship, just as some Christians regard Eucharistic worship in the same way. This may have the effect of making them feel free to join in other religious activities without any sense of compromise.

52   But perhaps it can at least be said that all religious traditions seem to have at least two styles of worship. One is a highly formalised, 'official' kind of set piece, or series of set pieces (which need not necessarily be congregational), usually conducted by a professional religious person, and often in a ritual language which is not the language of everyday – Hebrew, Arabic (used even for those who do not speak those languages), Sanskrit, Pali, and among Christians languages like Slavonic, Coptic, or even Latin. These 'set pieces' have a definite structure, which may only be varied in minor ways, and they usually take place in buildings like temples and mosques used largely or exclusively for those purposes. This is probably what most westerners would understand by the word 'worship'.

53   There is, however, a second and equally important style of worship which is much more informal, fluid and commonplace. It can be seen in the ritual exchanges of greeting when two people meet, which invoke God's blessing and peace on the life and families of each. Muslims begin many public functions with a reading from the Qur'an, or at least with a *b'ismillah* ('in the name of Allah') which serves as a kind of grace for many different activities. 786 is an Islamic numerical shorthand with the same meaning, used constantly on the doors of houses, on cars, and at the head of documents of every kind, even children's school essays. Hindus greet each other with *namaste*, which is understood as an acknowledgement of the divinity inhering one another, and among many different religious communities in India even adult sons and daughters may stoop to touch their parents' feet, symbolically putting themselves under those feet, while the parents respond with a hand on their heads in blessing.

54   The Sanskrit word *puja* is defined as 'honour, worship, respect, reverence, veneration, homage (to superiors), adoration (of gods)'. As in the 1662 Marriage service – 'with my body I thee worship' – it is quite clearly something given to human beings as well as to God. Hindu temple worship uses many of the ritual forms of behaviour which

originated as forms of respect to the king in the ancient royal courts of India, so it is not surprising if there is still a continuum of ritual or semi-ritual actions ranging from the respect due to a superior to that due to God. After all, 'Your Worship' is still a title used in Britain.

55   The significance of all this is that a modern, secular and avowedly egalitarian society finds it difficult to appreciate the extent to which life in much of the rest of the world is lived with a continual consciousness of the dimension of divinity. For many immersed in such traditions worship is therefore the most natural thing in the world, and sharing in what has been described here as the informal level of worship presents no problems at all. Generally speaking, the same would be true of more formal worship for Hindus and Sikhs, whereas Jews and Muslims would face difficulties wherever the use of any kind of image suggested idolatry.

Idols and Images

56   There is no doubt that Christian participation in multi-faith activities with elements of common worship will have attendant dangers. Christians will not wish to be involved in anything which could be construed as idolatry. However, it is not always recognised by Christians that Muslims and Jews in particular have the same, if not stronger, convictions about idolatry, and that many Sikhs and Hindus will share their views.

57   It is easier to denounce idolatry than to define it. Put simply, idolatry is the worship of something less than God. This may be an image of wood or stone which a worshipper kisses or bows before or makes offerings in front of; or it may be something like money, sex, power or the nation, which becomes the focal point of an individual or group's personality. The material image may be less dangerous, because so obviously not in itself divine, than the idea or the ideology. Worshippers who use images, for example the icons of Christian Orthodox tradition, usually insist that they are worshipping God through the image, and not the image itself.

58   It is almost certainly wise to avoid the use of any material image in worship designed for people from a number of religious traditions, since Muslims and Jews will object to it even if others do not.

59   Some Christians are likely to feel uneasy in their first visit to a Hindu temple because of the many unfamiliar images there. It is wise, however, to suspend judgement until it is possible to discover what the Hindus of that place themselves think the images are for. Even when Hindu worshippers appear to be identifying the images as themselves divine, allowances need to be made when people are trying to express sophisticated thoughts in their second language. If, however, Christians feel that they themselves are being drawn into idolatrous worship, it may be best for them to leave politely.

IV VISITING THE PLACES OF WORSHIP OF OTHER FAITHS

60   Many Anglicans have little experience of visiting even other Christian churches for worship, so that the idea of visiting a temple, synagogue or mosque may seem very strange to them. Yet as long ago as 1968 the British Council of Churches' report encouraged the creation of

> opportunities for Christians to exchange visits with those of other faiths for sympathetic and *instructed observation* of one another's *worship*.

61   *Worship* is fundamental to most faiths, so any attempt at mutual understanding must involve an attempt to appreciate each other's worship. Obviously, therefore, attendance at one another's worship is desirable before any more structured forms of worshipping together.

62   *Instructed*: There should be explanation before the visit of what will take place and its significance, with an opportunity to ask questions. It is important to show respect by complying with the normal pattern of behaviour of the faithful in their place of worship. Visitors should find out beforehand what participation, if any, might be expected of them in the worship that is offered, and work out what they can and cannot do with integrity. The adventure of faith may entail mistakes honestly made.

63   *Observation*: Where does observation end and participation begin? In some cases, visitors might find themselves feeling that they are worshipping inwardly; sometimes they might even feel able to participate in outward acts. It may be more difficult to feel that one is fully participating in worship when (as will usually be the case) it is conducted in a language one does not understand.

64   All believers like to feel that they can participate in worship, and to be allowed only to observe, as in the mosque, may be alienating. On the other hand participation, or the invitation to join in, can bring its own difficulties, as in the Hindu temple when hymns are sung to Krishna and the worshippers bow to Hanuman and Ganesh. The Christian visitors are welcome to join in, but can they in good conscience do so? What they decide may depend to a great extent on the

particular Christian tradition in which they have been nurtured, but in either case the question arises: 'What am I doing here? Am I simply invading the privacy of another people's world in order to satisfy my own curiosity? Worse, am I betraying my own faith even by being here?'

65   The fear of the intrusion on others' intimacy is fairly easily dealt with. Hardly anyone would go to another place of worship without an invitation to do so, or without making a request beforehand. But even if they did arrive entirely unannounced, experience in Britain suggests that visitors from outside the particular community of faith are invariably welcomed, provided they observe the simple courtesies of the place – which usually means removing your shoes and perhaps covering your head. Sikhs are inclined to say something along the lines of: 'This place belongs to you as much as it does to us. You are welcome here at any time. Don't think you have to ask beforehand.' But there are exceptions to this general welcome. The long and painful experience of Jewish people has made some of them more cautious than others, and even today attacks on synagogues are sadly not uncommon. In consequence Jews may be more wary of the non-Jewish outsider whom nobody in the congregation knows.

66   Whatever the particular circumstances of the place of worship, what goes on there is essentially a public act and not a private one, and is therefore in principle open to all. For Muslims in particular the five-times daily ritual prayer, and especially Friday prayer, is a statement of their basic identity as a servant of God which should never be concealed, and of which they could never be ashamed. As with other believers, their worship is a witness to the world, and they will be glad for it to be observed.

67   If it is not an intrusion for a Christian to visit another place of worship, is it nevertheless a pretence or even a betrayal? Here it is necessary to discriminate. In very broad and general terms, Jews and Muslims are well aware that they have fundamental differences of belief with Christians, and that it is pointless to pretend otherwise. Hindus, Sikhs, and some Buddhists, on the other hand, usually claim that all truly religious people are making the same journey by different routes, and that the heart of all faiths is the same. Does this mean that some kind of pretence that all faiths are the same is possible in the temple,

when it is not possible in the mosque or the synagogue? Do Christians by their mere presence in the temple give support to the idea that Christ is only one of many saviours? Some would say 'Yes', some 'No', and others 'It depends what they do there.' And is the visit to an otherwise empty place of worship compromising, or is it being present during the ritual of another faith which creates difficulties?[8]

68   Hindus and Sikhs believe that all truly religious people are making the same journey by different routes. This belief is most unlikely to be affected by the presence or absence of Christians in the temple, since it is a basic part of much contemporary thought in religions of Indian origin.

69   We hope that all Christians will be willing to meet with people of other faith communities for the purpose of mutual recognition, friendship and learning. We should not forget that in Britain the Hindu, Muslim and Sikh communities are frequently disadvantaged ethnic minority groups which suffer extensively from racial harassment and social ills such as unemployment and poor housing beyond the average for the white community. They can benefit from Christian acknowledgement and recognition that they exist, that they are devout religious people, and that they are significant parts of the total community. Visiting the temple or the mosque says all that more effectively than mere words and is itself a 'statement' of the good news of Christian care.

70   The Christian visitors also benefit by close observation of different ways of worship. Some of these customs, such as the removal of shoes and sitting on the floor to worship, are practised widely by Christians in other parts of the world. Others, such as the Muslim *wudu*, or washing before prayer, may give a new insight into the need for proper preparation for prayer and perhaps into the significance of Christian cleansing in baptism. Muslims in particular pray with their whole bodies in bowing and prostration. (The mosque or *masjid* is the place of *sajda* or prostration.) This may make Western Christians think again about their own highly cerebral and book-dependent traditions of worship. It is rare to see books in the hands of Hindu, Sikh or Muslim

---

[8] For a consideration of the theological issues, see Chapter III.

worshippers. The hospitality of the Sikh temple in particular, and the long hours for which it is open every day, make a sharp contrast with the restricted life and use of many English church buildings.

Practical Issues

71 The following detailed information may help to illustrate the questions discussed above.

The Synagogue

72 In Orthodox synagogues, men and women have to sit separately, sometimes on either side of the sanctuary or sometimes with the women sitting behind a screen or in a gallery. In Reformed and Liberal Synagogues they may sit together. Modest dress is required for both sexes: men and married women cover their heads. Sometimes paper hats are provided, but these are often difficult to keep on, so it is better to bring a proper hat.

The Mosque

73 Shoes are removed. Women should cover their heads (men may sometimes also be asked to do this) and they should dress with modesty (skirts well below the knees, or trousers, no low-cut blouses or dresses). They may be obliged to cover their legs and arms. Remember that here, and in the Gurdwara and Hindu Temple, one will be sitting on the floor, which can make some types of clothing uncomfortable or embarrassing. Check beforehand whether female members of the party will be expected to join the Muslim women, or whether they will be allowed to accompany the men. Muslims will not normally invite visitors to join the line for ritual prayer, but if this is done Christians will have to decide whether or not this implies total identification with the Islamic faith.

The Gurdwara

74 Women should dress modestly. Shoes must be removed and the head covered by men and women. No drugs, alcohol or tobacco should ever be taken into the Gurdwara. Sikhs make obeisance to the Guru Granth Sahib (sacred scriptures) as a mark of respect; Christians will not normally be expected to do this, but it would be appropriate to

stand before the book and not turn one's back on it in walking away. When sitting on the floor the soles of the feet should never be put facing the Guru Granth Sahib. As this is an insulting posture in Asia, it is better to sit cross-legged or with the feet behind. At the end of the service *Kara-parshad* (a semolina-based sweet) will be given to all. This sweetmeat has been made with special prayers and some Christians feel that they must politely refuse it. Others reckon that since Sikhs reject idolatry and the use of images, there need be no difficulty in accepting it. Sikhs regard it as a symbol of unity and equality.

The Hindu Temple

75   Shoes must be removed. Women might cover their heads, as Hindu women do. It is usually in the Hindu temple that difficulties with regard to participation in ceremonies arise. It is hard to be a detached observer. Hindus pay homage to the deities by bowing before them with their hands together; most Christians would not normally do this. At the *arati* ceremony an invitation would be given to pass the hand over the flame of the *arati* dish and to touch one's forehead with the hand, thus taking a blessing to oneself. The visitor may be expected to put a coin in the dish. On leaving, guests are normally offered *prasad* – sweetmeats, raisins, nuts or fruit which have been offered to God by placing them before one of the images. Some may thus regard *prasad* as 'food consecrated to idols' (cf. 1 Corinthians 8.10). Christians may consider that they can accept it, on the grounds that no idolatry is intended, and idols have no independent reality anyway; or pragmatically, that acceptance will advance relations whereas refusal may be misunderstood. Alternatively, Christians may want tactfully to decline the offer, believing that the custom is at best ambiguous, and is certainly likely to disturb converts to Christianity from Hinduism as well as implying that all religions are paths to the same end.[9]

The Buddhist Meditation Hall and Temple

76   In the meditation hall Christians may ask themselves whether they should acknowledge the Buddha's image. Some, respecting his message and influence, feel able to do so, even though some of their conclusions

---

[9] See the section on Idols and Images at the end of Chapter III.

differ. Chanting in the temple is more problematic. Sitting in the correct position for a considerable length of time is itself not easy, and if one is invited to offer incense before the image of the Buddha, how should one respond? Incense first came into the Christian Church as a mark of respect to imperial officers (such as the bishops became) and it need not be associated with deity. This might suggest that Christians could, on certain occasions, take part in the ritual with integrity. However, Christians who have only used incense in offering it to Christ in a Christian setting are likely to find it difficult to accept such an invitation, especially when they remember how Christians gave their lives rather than offer a pinch of incense to the Roman emperors who claimed deity. Seen in this context, offering incense before the Buddha's image is at best open to misinterpretation.

General points

77   Some practical points should be borne in mind:

Plenty of time should be allowed for the visit, and one should be prepared for refreshments, which may include very hot curry.

Places of worship of all faiths are often ill-equipped with toilets.

It is as well to avoid drinking alcohol before visiting a place of worship.

A deliberate decision to wear religious symbols or slogans such as 'Jesus saves' which are not normally worn can be tactless and offensive in the place of worship of another faith.

Some Considerations for Church Leaders

78   There are questions which have to be faced by the authorised representative of the Christian Church, the parish priest or deacon, and even more by the bishop.

79   Ordained ministers call the Church to be true to the Gospel of Christ. They do so aware of the different assumptions within the Church concerning the Gospel, the nature of the Church, and the task of leadership. Some Christians expect the clergy to work almost entirely within the Church, encouraging the whole people of God in their daily witness. They grow anxious if the clergy venture into a multi-faith context; they fear that the Gospel will be diluted, the clergy contaminated; they feel safer with clear boundaries between

Christianity and other faiths. For example, some ministers will be made more aware of the strong feelings possessed by those Christian communities who are happy for their leaders to visit 'neutral communities' such as a hospital or factory but become alarmed if they visit the meeting place of people of another faith. Other Christians hope that the clergy will spearhead the apostolic and pioneering work of the Church, and so establish relationships with people of other faiths.

80   Clergy in England are also familiar with the expectations of their rôle that arise from nominal Christians who do not belong to a worshipping Christian community, from non-believers, and from members of communities of another faith. People of other faiths or of no faith continue to hope that the Church and her representatives will exhibit and encourage the virtues of acceptance, toleration, peaceful co-existence and co-operation, encouraging a climate of opinion such that people of different faiths and persuasions can live distinctively and securely. And some ministers will discover the range of disappointment experienced by leaders and communities of other faiths if Christian leaders find persistent reason for being unable to recognise them and meet with them.

81   Before Christian ministers propose visiting a community of another faith or attending a 'multi-faith act of worship' they should ask what statement is being made by their presence at the meeting of another faith community or by their refusal to attend.

82   Ministers should as far as possible discover from their hosts what will be expected of them during the visit and indicate which of these expectations they will be able to meet. An address will often be expected. They will need to satisfy themselves that their presence will indicate awareness, friendship, and understanding of the faith community without identifying with the distinctive faith of that community.

V CHRISTIAN SERVICES ATTENDED BY PEOPLE OF OTHER FAITHS

83 Anglican services are open to all members of the public, and from time to time they are attended by people of other faiths and of little or no faith at all. For Christians there are no issues of principle involved in the fact that people of other faiths may attend a Christian service held in a Christian church.

84 People of other faiths may be present for different reasons. They may come unexpectedly to see what a Christian service is like, or they may be invited to attend for that purpose. Alternatively, one of the reasons for holding a multi-faith service listed in Chapter VI below may have prompted planning of a special Christian service in a Christian church but designed for a congregation including many people of other faiths. What is appropriate will vary according to the circumstances.

85 As with a visit by Christians to the place of worship of another faith, the visitors should be informed throughout about what will happen, and its significance. Freedom should be accorded to the guests to participate (by standing, kneeling, singing, etc.) or not, and explicit reference should be made to this before and during the service. Guests should not be placed in the front row, where they will not be able to see what the congregation is doing.

86 If people of other faiths are invited to attend the normal Sunday morning worship in a parish church, it will commonly be a Eucharist at which they are invited to be present. It is important that it is explained to them that they cannot be invited to receive the bread and wine, and why. Amongst others, Japanese Buddhists, for example, might otherwise present themselves for communion out of courtesy to their hosts. For them, identification with others in their religious activities is an act of politeness. If for any reason a form of service different from the usual one is chosen, then the guests should be informed that what is happening is not habitual for the Christian congregation.

87 There should be a genuine welcome for the guests as they arrive, and it is appropriate to offer hospitality afterwards. Enquiries should be made beforehand as to what the guests can and cannot eat and drink. If

a visit by a relatively small group is involved, someone can be designated to assist each guest through the service, remembering that they may not understand, or fully understand, the English language.

88   If people of other faiths are expected to attend there are several ways of responding in terms of what is done. This will depend partly on the purpose of the occasion.

Regular Christian Worship

89   If the guests are to experience regular Christian worship, then it may be decided not to make any special adaptation of the service, except that a public word of welcome may be appropriate.

Appropriate Christian Material specially selected

90   On the other hand, it may be felt appropriate to make a varying amount of adaptation. Sensitivity might be exercised in the choice of hymns and scripture readings. Prayers, hymns and readings might also be chosen for their readier intelligibility to people of other faiths.

91   Going further, it might be decided positively to select material whose message is acceptable to all. Examples might be hymns such as 'Immortal, invisible, God only wise' and lessons such as 1 Corinthians 13. However, if the occasion is supposed to be an opportunity for guests to experience an act of Christian worship, it would not be appropriate to make the whole service of this nature. Since Anglican services are normally liturgical, it would be most natural for one of the authorized liturgies to be followed.

92   This type of service might also be held in other circumstances, for reasons other than to enable visitors to experience Christian worship. In such a case, the service would be a Christian service designed to be as 'inclusive' and widely acceptable as possible. A specially-constructed order of service would then also include prayers couched in generally acceptable terms.

93   However, if the service is to be a Christian service, that suggests that there will be certain specifically Christian features which make it so. For example, Christians normally pray 'Through Jesus Christ our

Lord'. A service in which the name of Christ was not mentioned could hardly be described as an act of Christian worship.

94   This sort of service can also be seen as patronising, in that it seeks to be 'multi-faith' in content as well as in its congregation, but retains a Christian form and makes use only of Christian material and ministers.

Material from non-Christian Sources included

95   A further variation is the inclusion of material from non-Christian sources. This is still a Christian service, and all who lead it are Christians, but material from other faiths is included. Again, the purpose of such a service could not be to enable guests to experience normal Christian worship. One reason for the inclusion of such material might be to enrich the experience of the Christian congregation. Such additional material would doubtless be valuable, but in the case of lections it may be necessary to ask whether they are being read as 'the Word of God', and whether they are adding to or replacing readings from the Bible.

96   Another reason for including such material would be as a further way of making a Christian service held on a particular occasion or for a special reason as 'inclusive' and accessible as possible to people of other faiths. Again this could be regarded as patronising for the additional reason that if the texts are chosen by Christian ministers, or by the guests but on the ministers' advice, this may mean more or less consciously shaping the witness of other faiths to what seems compatible with the Christian view.

97   There is much in the scriptures of other faiths and in their liturgies which could be used in such a service. Obviously, if the service is to be an act of Christian worship, then it is to be expected that none of the material used would be contrary to the Christian faith.

Guest Participants from other Faiths

98   It is but a small step from a Christian service led by Christians, but incorporating material from other faiths, to inviting representatives of

other faiths to present the material themselves, if they feel able to do so in conscience. It must be recognised that this would mean their explicit and public participation in a service which might contain elements contrary to their own convictions.

99   One idea which might occur is to invite someone of another faith to preach at a Christian service. This is very problematic, however. In 1989 controversy was caused by an invitation being extended to a rabbi to preach at matins in an English Cathedral; the fact that the Sunday concerned was Trinity Sunday only complicated the issue. Someone of another faith might profitably be invited to give an address in a church, but it is hard to see how such a person can preach the Gospel during an act of Christian worship. One way of proceeding would be to conclude the service, inviting the congregation to remain to hear an address after a break, but such an address should be in addition to, not in place of, the sermon, if the service is one at which a sermon would otherwise have been preached.

VI 'MULTI-FAITH WORSHIP' – WHY, WHO AND WHERE?

100 Churches do not only pursue their regular pattern of services. Most ministers find themselves asked at some time if their church may be used for a special service. This may be in celebration or in commemoration, or at a time of crisis. Nowadays when the arrangements are being made it not infrequently happens that there is a request for at least some minimal recognition of religious traditions other than the Christian. This chapter offers some reflection on the purpose of such services, the people who will attend and lead them, and appropriate venues.

WHY?

What are the reasons for gathering for 'multi-faith worship', and for whom is the occasion designed?

101 It often happens that those who request some kind of 'multi-faith worship' ask for a 'multi-cultural' emphasis, and, reflecting secular usage, do not distinguish between what is multi-cultural and what is multi-faith. Unless they are deeply religious people themselves they may not anticipate that any problems of belief will be involved, and may be rather surprised to discover that for some people at least, they are. Taking one of the examples given in Chapter I, those responsible for organising a special service for scouts may ask the church or cathedral authorities to bear in mind that it would be nice if some Muslim or Hindu prayers could be included. For such a group, the relevant community consists of those people drawn together by scouting or some other special interest, and not the people who worship God in Christ. To refuse any accommodation to their request may be to run the risk of appearing to exclude some members of the movement on the basis of their race or culture. Racism, after all, is more widely encountered than theological scruple.

102 Occasions of 'multi-faith worship' are not ends in themselves. Those planning such occasions should be clear about the reasons for holding them. An important factor is the nature of the congregation expected to attend. The questions and suggestions in this chapter might lead to the conclusion that a 'multi-faith service' is not appropriate in a

particular case or at a particular time, or that one of the types of multi-faith event described in later chapters might be more appropriate for the occasion in question than another.

103   Clearly it is important that if the occasion is to be multi-faith, the congregation is itself made up of people of different faiths. In general, 'multi-faith worship' will be more appropriate if the congregation already forms, or feels part of, a single, multi-faith *community* before the service, especially if those present already form a *fellowship* of people who know, respect and trust each other. It will also be more appropriate and successful where those present are genuinely united by a *shared concern*. The extent to which community, fellowship and shared concern are present, together with the particular combination of faiths which are represented, will determine what can and should be done.

104   Some examples of the types of situation which lead people to plan 'multi-faith services' follow. Most of them display these features of community, fellowship and shared concern, but to different degrees.

An Observance for Commonwealth Day

105   Those attending this annual occasion in Westminster Abbey have in common their citizenship of member states of the Commonwealth. The Observance intends to celebrate and deepen the sense of community and give ritual and symbolic expression to the shared ideals of the Commonwealth.

Civic and National Services

106   Multi-faith civic services are often held in areas populated by many people of different faiths simply to enable citizens to pray together for the community. An example of this is an annual mayoral service, such as a multi-faith mayoral service held in Bedford in 1989. On the other hand, services may be organised by or on behalf of a civic community as a result of an event such as a tragedy like the fire at Bradford City football ground in 1985. Some of these events have the status of national disasters. In such cases there is a heightened sense of community, and a shared concern to mourn. People of many faiths may have been involved in the tragedy, and if so, a multi-faith observance may be very appropriate. Services are also organised to celebrate national events, or local events such as a civic anniversary. On such

occasions it is joy rather than sorrow which produces a heightened sense of community, and there is a shared concern to rejoice and celebrate.

Services for Individual Organisations

107 Sometimes organisations wish to organise services for their members. These may be international, national, county or local services. Those present have in common both their membership of the organisation and shared ideals and concerns which are stronger than is the case in many civic events. In some cases there may also be a real fellowship between members of the congregation whose individual faith commitments differ.

Conferences and similar Events

108 When people of different faiths are present at a conference or similar event, it may be desired that services held should be multi-faith. Those present may be members of the same organisation and may already know each other, and the theme of the conference may give rise to a shared concern. During a conference a feeling of fellowship develops between participants, who may get to know, respect and trust each other more quickly than is usual. For this reason a 'multi-faith service' may be more appropriate at the end of the conference than at the beginning.

Services organised by Local Interfaith Groups

109 This single heading covers a variety of very different types of service. The service may be organised for members of a local dialogue group only. Often it will only be after months, maybe even years, of meeting together that the group feels able to move towards praying together. By then the group will have become a community, even a fellowship, marked by mutual respect and trust, and will probably have shared concerns.* Local interfaith groups are one type of group which organises services based on particular shared concerns, discussed below.

---

* A description of this process is given by Andrew Wingate in *Encounter in the Spirit* (Risk Series, No. 39, WCC, 1988).

Services for Particular Concerns

110   Sometimes services are organised by individuals, groups or organisations, including churches or faith communities, in order to express a particular concern. Shared concerns include, for example, concern for Peace, Justice, World Unity or the Environment, as well as more specific campaigns. Such occasions have clear advantages; the participants are united by a shared concern; there is a clear theme for the service, and often a wealth of material from which to choose.

111   However, there are also difficulties which have to be faced. In some cases the members of the congregations will neither be known to each other, nor have any community membership in common beyond their common membership of the human race. Unlike some of the other shared concerns which have been mentioned in this chapter, these concerns may not be as commonly held as might be supposed. Do people of the faiths represented really mean the same when they speak of concepts such as peace and justice? (cf. *Can We Pray Together?*, p.7) If the service proceeds from general notions to specific instances, will all be in agreement? On the other hand, the more general the concern, the greater the danger that it will become vague, nebulous and bland.

112   When the concern underlying a service is itself controversial (for example multi-faith prayer 'for the imposition of sanctions against South Africa' or 'for unilateral nuclear disarmament'), this could add to the problems. Whenever a service is held in support of a political cause the minister has to consider whether the Church would be seen to be taking sides, but this is particularly true in the case of 'multi-faith services'. The controversy to which such services not infrequently give rise would be increased by the choice of such a theme. The danger of doing anything which might cause 'multi-faith services' to be surrounded by additional controversy and to become associated with causes which are divisive needs to be weighed.

113   The 'concern' may be problematic without being political. It may be contrary to the Christian faith, designed to espouse the notion that all religions are the same, or to promote a new 'interfaith' religion composed of a collection of elements from many religions or a lowest common denominator of them all. That would be quite different from people who recognise that they have different faiths nevertheless doing what they can in conscience together.

114   Services relating to environmental concerns may pose specific problems of their own. When attention is focused on the created order, there may be a danger that worship of the Creator is neglected and creatures, even the earth itself, are reverenced to the point where they are addressed in prayer and, indeed, worshipped. This would be clearly contrary to the Christian faith and to many other faiths.

WHO?

Is every group welcome to participate?

115   Some discernment is required in the question of who will attend and participate in the service. Where the service is open to the public (as would normally be the case), people of any persuasion or none are welcome to attend. However, when it comes to participation in the leadership of the service, for example by reading, other considerations come into play. Christians would wish to be represented by a member of a mainstream Christian denomination. Similarly, members of other faiths would not expect to be represented by members of breakaway groups. Without detailed knowledge of other faith communities it is sometimes difficult to ascertain which leaders are genuinely representative of certain local communities.

116   Where members of New Religious Movements[10] are to participate in their own right, the problems are more difficult. Should boundaries be drawn, and if so, where and by whom? It is possible that some groups will not attend if members of certain sects or movements are to participate.

WHERE?

Where will the service take place?

117   The venue for a 'multi-faith service' could be a church, a church hall, a secular building, an open-air site or the place of worship of another faith.

---

[10]   See E. Barker, *New Religious Movements: A Practical Introduction* (HMSO, 1989).

118   The first instinct of many Christians will be to hold such services in a church. The Church of England has a large number of buildings, many of them bigger than others which might be available, but it is also because of the national position of the Church of England that many feel it appropriate to hold services designed for the whole community in what is still often one of the community's focal points. By making its building available, the Church is showing hospitality and giving a welcome to people of other faiths.

119   However, if the service is held in an Anglican church it must comply with the requirements of Canon Law.[11] It is also important to remember that Anglican parish churches, and even more so cathedrals, as well as being focal points for the whole community, including people of other faiths, are also especially focal points for the wider Christian community including Christians of other denominations. They are symbols for the Christian faith. In particular, a cathedral is the church of the bishop and thus the mother church of the diocese. Individual Anglican churches, as well as belonging to the Church of England, belong to the worldwide Anglican Communion. Those planning to hold 'multi-faith services' in parish churches and particularly in cathedrals need to be sensitive not only to the feelings of people of other faiths but also to those of the wider Anglican and Christian community of the parish or diocese, and even to those of Anglicans in other dioceses and Anglican Churches.

120   Many consider that people of different faiths cannot meet on equal terms unless they meet on neutral ground. Anglican churches have crosses and other Christian symbols, which will be foreign to all people of other faiths and objectionable to some. It might be suggested that such symbols should be covered or removed. But this would be to attempt to turn a church into that which it is not; a church is not and cannot be 'neutral ground'; indeed members of other faith communities would not expect it to be other than it is.

121   Some of the same considerations apply to non-Anglican churches. Although they are not subject to Anglican Canon Law, they are subject to the rules of the church concerned and may be covered by restrictive trust deeds.

---

[11] See Chapter IX.

122   There may be no secular hall of suitable size available, but even if there is, many will feel that it does not have the 'numinous atmosphere' of a building set aside for worship which is fitting for joint worship. On the other hand the use of non-religious buildings for multi-faith services avoids many of the difficulties which the use of churches may pose. They are 'neutral ground', and may be arranged more flexibly than is often the case with a church. Larger numbers of people may often be accommodated at open air events (although it may rain!).

VII 'SERIAL MULTI-FAITH SERVICES'

123   If Christians may be present at the worship of other faiths and people of other faiths may be present at Christian worship (as suggested in Chapters IV and V), could this 'being present' at each other's worship be combined in a single event? This would seem to be a way of meeting, with integrity, the need for 'multi-faith services' which is felt in particular situations and contexts.[12]

124   Such an event has been described as a 'serial multi-faith service'. As long ago as 1968 the British Council of Churches report encouraged the exploration of such occasions.[13] In them, Christians are present at acts of worship of other faiths, and people of other faiths are present at a Christian act of worship. Each brief act of worship is separate and complete in itself, and each involves 'what is characteristic' of the faith concerned. These separate contributions are distinct entities, for which the other faiths have no implied responsibility. In such services each community is responsible for the selection and presentation of its own material. Those present share in the worship of faiths other than their own only as far as they feel able to do so and can understand what is happening.

125   The BCC report envisaged that 'These shared observances would include both a clear testimony to the saving work of God in Christ and sympathetic listening to the testimony of other faiths'. Those present might not be praying together, but they would be praying in each other's presence. Such events provide an opportunity to 'celebrate togetherness'; meeting flows into the realm of worship.

126   If there is a clear occasion for the service this gives a rationale for what happens. Each faith group offers to God and to the others something which is important to it. The cohesion of the event is even more likely to be enhanced when there is a common theme running through the material presented, and a common intention for the prayers (for example, prayer for peace).

---

[12] See Chapters I and VI.
[13] See Chapter II.

127   If there is no clear occasion, common theme or intention, the event may seem like a disjointed series of 'slots'. Unless care is taken, each contribution can become a 'show piece' to be performed in front of the other groups.

128   On the other hand, if the separate contributions are integrated too much, it may be difficult to make the distinction between the acts of worship clear. This would apply especially if the event were held in the place of worship of one of the faiths involved, rather than in a 'neutral' place. It might be difficult to avoid the impression the worship of the other faiths is being absorbed into the worship of the 'host' faith.

129   Is it appropriate for a Christian, and especially a Christian minister, to participate in such events? As they are the combination of attending the worship of other faiths and receiving visitors to Christian worship, the same considerations apply.[14]

130   However, additional issues arise when the visits are combined into one event. The most important issue is that of venue. It is neither appropriate nor lawful for words or actions which are contrary to the Christian faith to be performed in an Anglican church. If each community is responsible for the selection and presentation of its own material, and if each brief act of worship involves what is characteristic of the faith concerned, the other communities having no implied responsibility for it, it is hard to see how such an event could be held in an Anglican Church. By definition, the minister would have no control over what took place, even though there might be some liaison.

131   A neutral venue also has disadvantages, however.[15] If the places of worship of the different faith communities involved are close enough to each other, the ideal solution may be a multi-faith pilgrimage. Each community can offer its own brief act of worship in the context of its own place of worship, the congregation processing from place to place. An example of this is the service and pilgrimage held to launch the 1989 International Week of Prayer for World Peace in Coventry. Prayers were held in the Chapel of Unity at the Cathedral and then in the Mosque, Hindu temple and Gurdwara nearby. An annual multi-faith pilgrimage in London follows a similar pattern.

---

[14]   See Chapters IV and V.
[15]   See Chapter VI.

VIII 'MULTI-FAITH SERVICES WITH AN AGREED COMMON ORDER'

132   Some have wished to go beyond being present at each other's worship, whether by visits and hospitality or through a 'serial multi-faith service'.[16] In view of all that is shared by people of different faiths, they have felt able to arrange multi-faith events with an order of service whose contents are agreed by all the participating faith communities, in which all that is done is seen as part of a single, common observance or celebration.

133   The 'multi-faith service with an agreed common order' is the type of activity which most readily springs to mind when 'multi-faith worship' is mentioned. It was pioneered by the World Congress of Faiths. The 1979 report of the Archbishops' Consultants encouraged 'Christians who are able in good conscience to do so to take part in such services'.

134   Within this type of service there is a range of possibilities. Material from the different faiths may always be contributed by representatives of the faith concerned. If this principle is strictly adhered to, the only difference from the 'serial multi-faith service' is the fact that there is an agreed common order instead of a series of brief but distinct acts of worship. Some of the comments made about that type of service are relevant.

135   However, it is usual for some common material to be provided for congregational participation, such as hymns or affirmations. The hymns are often of Christian origin, but containing sentiments which are more widely acceptable. An example of this type of service is the Observance for Commonwealth Day held each year in Westminster Abbey.

136   Going further, all of the material may be common. In this case

---

[16]   See Chapters IV, V and VII.

there is no insistence that items are contributed by representatives of the tradition from which they come. The possibility of disjointedness is overcome, and the items are less likely to seem like performances, but the risk of giving the impression that all religions are one is increased. Nevertheless, such services can be constructed in such a way that all can participate with integrity.

137   In some cases, however, items from a variety of sources seem to have been blended together with little concern for their original meaning or intention, either carelessly, or with enthusiasm to create a sense of harmony. In this case, no awareness is shown of the theological implications of what is being done. At its worst, such a service might positively be intended to express the view that 'we are all one', suggesting a new interfaith religion.

Points for Consideration

138   Some feel that the type of service described in this chapter is not appropriate for civic, national or international public occasions, since many of those who attend would not be in a position to recognise the difference between the faiths, and likely reporting by the media would tend to confirm the widespread view of members of the public that religions are in the end much the same, while strengthening the resistance of many Christians to any form of 'multi-faith worship'. In any such service it is likely that all that is distinctive of the different faiths, particularly their ritual, will be discarded. What remains may seem empty, bland or insipid.

139   Also, such services may tend in practice to approximate to the familiar pattern of Christian worship; often they are epecially reminiscent of a certain form of non-liturgical service. Frequently use of lections from different religions is envisaged, and it seems likely that this is due to the fact that lections form an integral part of Christian worship. The assumption that the use of lections is equally a part of the tradition of others needs to be questioned; even when the other faiths do use lections in worship, this may not be the most typical aspect of worship for them. The differences in the approach to worship of the different faiths are even more fundamental. For example, both Sikhs and Hindus make offerings, and the food offered then becomes the *prasad* which is shared by the community. Is a service worship for them,

where there is no *prasad*?[17] If such services take place in Anglican churches Christian domination is even more apparent.[18]

140   In what follows we offer some principles for those who decide to plan a service of this type to bear in mind, and consider some of the types of material which are often included. Much of what we say here applies also to the types of service described in earlier sections.

Principles

141   The purpose of the occasion should be made clear in an introduction.[19]

142   Items should be selected to emphasise what all present hold in common, but without glossing over differences or giving the impression that none exist. Nevertheless, it is important to remember that presence at a service does not necessarily imply total assent to all that is said or done.

143   The meaning of intended actions should be made clear at the service. There should also be no deliberate ambiguity or blurring of meaning, such that participants are expected, implicitly or explicitly, to interpret words or actions in contradictory ways. Words or actions should not be used with an intention radically different from their original or normal purpose.

144   Those attending such a service should not be asked to do things which many will feel they cannot do with integrity. People should not feel that they are being pushed into doing something for which they do not feel ready. If there is an invitation to do something, it should be couched in terms which mean that those who do not feel able to join in do not feel embarrassed or excluded.

145   If parts of the service are to be in a language other than English, where possible a written translation should be available. Where a

---

[17] See paragraphs 51 and 74-5 above.
[18] See paragraphs 120-1 above.
[19] See Chapter IV.

sizable proportion of members of one or more of the faith communities likely to attend do not understand English, translations should similarly be made available.

146   The desire to involve all should not be taken to such lengths that the service becomes interminably protracted.

Planning and Evaluation

147   All these principles make careful planning of the service necessary. This provides an opportunity for consultation with representatives of all the faith communities which are to participate. This will also avoid *needless* offence. Some 'offence' is inevitable, in the sense that, for example, reference to Christ as 'our Lord' by Christians may be 'offensive' to others, but careful planning will at least avoid unintentional offence resulting from ignorance.

148   In their participation in such services, Christians should avoid giving the impression that Jesus Christ is merely one of many saviours. Christian contributors need not be embarrassed by mentioning the Name of Christ. Services in which Christians participate, but in which Christ is not mentioned at all, understandably give offence to many Christians.

149   It must, however, be recognised that some will be opposed to such services, even offended by them. The planners would be well advised to explain their intentions and plans to likely objectors well in advance. It may be possible to reassure those who are alarmed, and if not, controversy is at least likely to be based on the facts, rather than on rumour or misunderstanding. Care should be taken to avoid *needless* offence.

150   Publicity should be planned carefully, both to encourage people to attend, and to avoid creating misleading impressions. Careful consideration should be given to the term used to describe the occasion, although this may not make much difference to the legal constraints if the service is to take place in an Anglican church. There is a need to describe honestly what is intended. The use of a distinctive term might make it clear that the event is not intended to be part of the normal programme of worship.

151   It is important to evaluate the event afterwards. Future events can then be planned in the light of what has been learned (although the fact that one event has been 'successful' should not in itself be taken as a reason for organising another, simply because 'it worked before'.[20] The evaluation should not only take account of the feelings of those who were present.

Types of Material

Readings

152   In addition to passages from the classical scriptures, appropriate poetry or poems might be chosen. Brief opening sentences may provide coherence to the whole. Attention needs to be given to the length, order and language of the readings.

Hymns

153   Where possible, these should not only come from the Christian tradition. Sometimes songs which do not explicitly refer to any religious tradition may nevertheless be appropriate to the theme.

154   Where a hymn is part of the Christian 'contribution' to the service, Christocentric hymns are not inappropriate since people of other faiths might expect Christian hymnody to make reference to Jesus Christ. However, when all are expected to join in singing a hymn from the Christian tradition, it should be one which is more widely acceptable – more theocentric and less Christocentric.

155   There is a danger that a very limited list of hymns, covering a very limited range of topics, is used at such services, and this becomes tedious if the services are held regularly.

156   The alteration of hymns in order to remove references to Christ, against the original intention of the authors, is not acceptable.

An Address

157   An introduction or address should make plain the purpose of the occasion and the basis on which people have come together. The content will be indicated by the theme and purpose of the occasion.

---

[20]   See Chapter VI.

Prayers

158   Prayers may come from a particular tradition or be universal in intention. It may be appropriate for the congregation to join in saying a prayer such as that attributed to St Francis of Assisi or another of similarly wide acceptability. The questions raised by praying together are at the heart of the whole question of 'multi-faith worship'.

Silence and Music

159   Silence gives all the opportunity to pray together, without one group imposing its way of praying on others. Each can ponder upon the common concern in their own way. The use of silence is highly recommended. (See *Can We Pray Together?*, pp. 17-19.) Music without words can also be a valuable aid to meditation.

Joint Affirmations

160   Joint affirmations offer those present the opportunity to affirm the values and aspirations they have in common, but here the dangers of syncretism and colourless platitude attend. The former seems to lurk in a description quoted in *Inter-faith Worship* (1974): 'A credo of a universal quality was spoken.' Such affirmations should not give the impression that they are substitutes for the credal statements of the various faiths. Blandness is also to some extent a matter of impressions. What appears platitudinous on paper may seem full of meaning in the context and atmosphere of a service in which it is spoken by a whole congregation.

Symbolic actions

161   Reference has already been made to the care with which symbolic actions need to be planned. Examples might be the lighting of candles or the giving of flowers, and the exchange of appropriate greetings (a greeting of 'Peace be with you' is common to many traditions, even if there are differences in understanding). Such symbolic actions are highly desirable. Most worship involves actions, and as a result, services which include no action may be unsatisfactory. Such actions also help to avoid the impression that the event is essentially a Christian service of the 'hymn sandwich' variety. A service consisting only of words spoken or sung is liable to be very cerebral and it is difficult for many to feel fully involved in such services.

IX THE LEGAL POSITION

162   Those planning multi-faith services should be aware of those provisions of the present Canons which affect 'multi-faith worship'. It is the responsibility of others to issue Judgements and Opinions. This chapter has been written on the basis of legal advice supplied by the General Synod's Legal Adviser, but it is not intended to be a definitive statement of the law.

Services in Anglican Places of Worship

163   Worship and other events held in a Church of England place of worship are governed by the Canon Law of the Church of England. A building and its curtilage which have been consecrated are said, in the deed of consecration, to be set apart for worship according to the rites and ceremonies of the Church of England for ever. In addition, worship and other activities in dedicated places of worship and consecrated churchyards and on land which is not consecrated but which is subject to the faculty jurisdiction are also subject to ecclesiastical law.

164   There is provision in Canon B4 for the Convocations or the Archbishops or the Ordinary to approve forms of service for occasions for which no provision is made in the *Book of Common Prayer* or by the General Synod (for example in the *Alternative Service Book*). Thus, where no service has been authorised nationally or for a whole province for particular occasions, the diocesan bishop may authorise a service for use in churches in his diocese. Where no such provision has been made, Canon B5 permits the minister to 'use forms of service considered suitable by him for those occasions'. In the case of forms of service authorised by the bishop, he must be satisfied that

> in words and order (the forms of service) are reverent and seemly and are neither contrary to, nor indicative of any departure from, the doctrine of the Church of England in any essential matter.

Substantially the same test applies in the case of forms of service authorised by the minister. If any question is raised under Canon B5 as to whether a form of service is consonant with the doctrine of the Church of England, it may be referred to the bishop for his 'pastoral guidance and advice'. These Canons apply to cathedral churches as well as to parish churches.

165   It is sometimes supposed that the requirements of Canon Law can be avoided by describing an occasion as 'a Celebration' or 'an Observance', but this is not so. Canon F16 requires that in the case of any 'play concert or exhibition of films or pictures' in a church or chapel the minister must take care

> that the words, music, and pictures are such as befit the House of God, are consonant with sound doctrine, and make for the edifying of the people.

If a multi-faith event involving words, music or pictures is not a service, then it is likely to be held to be a play, concert or exhibition under Canon F16. The requirement that the words, music and pictures must be 'consonant with sound doctrine' is similar to that for services, and if any doubt arises as to this it is to be referred to the bishop for his directions.

Services held elsewhere

166   The Canons, which in general date from some forty years ago, do not deal specifically with multi-faith events. However, Anglican clergy and other ministers who participate in the offering of public prayer in the course of such events remain bound by the Declaration of Assent contained in Canon C15, by which they promise that:

> in public prayer and administration of the sacraments, I will use only the forms of service which are authorised or allowed by Canons.

This means that they must comply with the provisions of Canon B5, set out above. (Deaconesses, readers and those admitted as lay workers all make a similar declaration as regards public prayer.)

167   In addition, Canon C26 provides that:

> A minister shall not give himself to such occupations, habits and recreations as do not befit his sacred calling, or may be detrimental to the performance of the duties of his office, or tend to be a just cause of offence to others; and at all times he shall be diligent to frame and fashion his life ... according to the doctrine of Christ...

168   In the absence of any specific guidance in the Canons, it is suggested that the test to be applied is whether, by what the Anglican clergyman or minister concerned does or says at the multi-faith event, he could reasonably be seen as associating himself with or assenting to doctrines inconsistent with those of the Christian Church in general or the Church of England in particular. In applying this test a number of factors may need to be taken into account, in addition to the form of the event itself and the words used; for example, whether the Anglican clergyman or minister is expected to robe, whether the event is taking place in a place of worship of another faith, whether it forms part of or is set in the context of an act of worship or ceremony of another faith, and what response, if any, is expected of Christians during or after non-Christian prayers or other non-Christian elements in the event.

169   It would be for the bishop to decide whether action should go forward under the legislation relating to clergy discipline in the event of a conflict with the Canons set out above. In any case, it is advisable for a member of the clergy to seek his bishop's goodwill in advance for participation in a multi-faith event.

170   Finally, where an Anglican priest or deacon is invited to take part publicly in 'multi-faith worship', in his capacity as a member of the Anglican clergy, he should bear in mind the normal requirement to respect parish boundaries contained in Canon C8, under which

> No minister who has ... authority to exercise his ministry in a diocese shall do so therein in any place in which he has not the cure of souls without the permission of the minister having such cure...

BIBLIOGRAPHY

A Publications mentioned in the text

A Statement on Inter-Faith Services (British Council of Churches, 1968)

M. Braybrooke (ed.), *Inter-faith Worship* (Galliard, 1974)

P.R. Akehurst and R.W.F. Wootton, *Inter-Faith Worship?* (Grove Booklet on Ministry and Worship No. 52, 1977)

Report of a Working Group on Interfaith Services and Worship (Archbishops' Interfaith Consultants), published in *Ends and Odds*, No. 22 (March 1980)

Relations with People of Other Faiths: Guidelines for Dialogue in Britain (Committee for Relations with People of Other Faiths, BCC, 1981/ 1983)

Can We Pray Together? Guidelines on Worship in a Multi-Faith Society (Committee for Relations with People of Other Faiths, BCC, 1983)

D. Bookless, *Interfaith Worship and Christian Truth* (Grove Worship Series, No. 117, 1991)

Towards a Theology for Inter-Faith Dialogue (Inter-Faith Consultative Group; Church House Publishing, 1984, 1986)

L. Newbigin, *The Gospel in a Pluralist Society* (SPCK, 1989)

K. Cracknell, *Towards a New Relationship* (Epworth Press, 1986)

J. Hick, *God Has Many Names* (Macmillan, 1980)

J. Hick, *An Interpretation of Religion* (Macmillan, 1989)

H. H. Rowley, *The Missionary Message of the Old Testament* (Oxford, 1945)

A. Wingate, *Encounter in the Spirit* (Risk series, No. 39, WCC, 1988)

E. Barker, *New Religious Movements: A Practical Introduction* (HMSO, 1989)

The Canons of the Church of England (Church House Publishing, 4th edition, 1986)

B Other relevant publications: a selection

M. Braybrooke, 'Inter-Faith Worship' in J. E. Davies (ed.), *A New Dictionary of Liturgy and Worship* (SCM, 1986)

'Interfaith Worship: Counsel for Lutherans' (Lutheran Council in the USA, 1986), published in *Current Dialogue*, xii (June 1987)

Our Ministry and Other Faiths (Hospital Chaplaincies Council, Church House Publishing, 1983

Handbook on Hospital Chaplaincy (Church House Publishing, 1987)

C Resources for Interfaith Worship: a selection

I A SELECTION OF MULTI-FAITH ASSEMBLY BOOKS

Although this booklet does not attempt to discuss worship in schools, the following material designed for use in schools may also be of general use.

L. Baker, *Secondary Assembly Notes* (Foulsham & Co, 1989)

R. Brandling, *Focus* (Bell & Hyman, 1983)

R. Brandling, *First Focus* (Bell & Hyman/Collins, 1984)

R. Brandling, *Assembly News* (Edward Arnold/Hodder & Stoughton, 1989)

R. Fisher, *The Assembly Year* (Collins, 1985)

J. Fitzsimmon & R. Whiteford, *Assemblies: Blueprints series* (Stanley Thornes, 1989)

W. Griffin, *Exploring Primary Assemblies* (Macmillan, 1984)

L. & M. Hoy, *Alternative Assembly Book* (Longman, 1985)

D. Moss, *A Word for Your Year* (Collins, 1986)

R. Profitt & V. Bishop, *Hand in Hand Assembly Book* (Longman, 1983)

T. Rousell, *Our Turn for Assembly* (Blackwell, 1985)

D. Self (ed.), *Lower School Assembly Book* (Hutchinson/Stanley Thornes), 1987

H. Smith, *Assemblies* (Heinemann Edn, 1981)

J. Tillman, *Oxford Assembly Book* (OUP, 1989)

J. Thompson, *Reflecting* (Edward Arnold/Hodder & Stoughton, 1988)

II GENERAL

G. Appleton (ed.), *The Oxford Book of Prayer* (OUP, 1988)

D. Faivre, *Prayer of Hope of an Interfaith Man* (BFSS National RE Centre, 1989) BFSS National RE Centre, West London Institute of Higher Education, Lancaster House, Borough Road, Isleworth, Middx TW7 5DU.

Westminster Interfaith Team, *Resources for Inter-faith Worship and Catechesis* (Westminster Interfaith Programme, 110 Thornbury Road, Osterley, Middx, TW7 4NN).

Week of Prayer for World Peace Prayer Leaflets (available from WPWP, Revd. Jonathan Blake, The Vicarage, 93 Pelham Road, Barnehurst, Bexleyheath DA7 4LY).

D   Annotated General Bibliography on Interfaith Dialogue

This bibliography supplements that given in the 1986 edition of *Towards a Theology for Inter-Faith Dialogue*.

Tosh Arai & Wesley Ariarajah (eds), *Spirituality in Interfaith Dialogue* (WCC, 1989). Ecumenical account of how different practitioners of dialogue have deepened their own Christian journey in the light of encountering the Spirit dwelling within other faiths.

Michael Barnes, *Religions in Conversation* (SPCK, 1989). Arguing for a broader approach to understanding the relationship between the religions than the usual categories, and taking seriously the role of the Holy Spirit.

Denise and John Carmody, *Prayer in World Religions* (Orbis, 1990). Descriptive accounts of prayer in Judaism, Islam, Hinduism, Buddhism, Native American and African Religions, together with a Christian response noting the common ground and differences.

Harvey Cox, *Many Mansions. A Christian's Encounter with Other Faiths* (Collins, 1988). Speaking from experience, a highly readable account of one man's reflections in the light of new encounters with people of other religions.

Gavin D'Costa (ed.), *Christian Uniqueness Reconsidered. The Myth of a Pluralistic Theology of Religions* (Orbis, 1990). In response to a growing acceptance of a pluralist view in the theology of religions, fourteen scholars challenge the assumptions that Christian faith is one among many when it comes to questions of salvation and truth.

Martin Forward (ed.), *God of All Faith. Discerning God's Presence in a Multi-Faith Society*, (Methodist Church Home Mission Divison, 1989). A collection of contributions by members of the Methodist Committee for Relations with People of Other Faiths, with questions and suggestions for group discussion.

Chester Gillis, *A Question of Final Belief. John Hick's Pluralistic Theory of Salvation* (Macmillan, 1989). Critical survey of Hick's development of his pluralistic hypothesis for interpreting global life. Covering epistemology, christology, soteriology.

Paul J. Griffiths, *Christianity through Non-Christian Eyes* (Orbis, 1990). A sobering account of how Christian faith often strikes people from the religious traditions.

John Hick, *Problems of Religious Pluralism* (Macmillan, 1985). A collection of essays responding to critics, exploring further the possibility of grading religions and the clash between truth-claims.

John Hick, *An Interpretation of Religion. Human Responses to the Transcendent* (Macmillan, 1989). Most up-to-date and sophisticated defence of Hick's pluralist model of the world's religious life. A *magnum opus*, it modifies some earlier statements.

John Hick & Paul Knitter (eds), *The Myth of Christian Uniqueness. Toward a Pluralistic Theology of Religions* (Orbis, 1987). Different reasons and routes for 'crossing the theological rubicon' where different faiths can be independent and valid approaches to the Truth.

John Hick & Edmunds Meltzer, *The Faiths – One God. A Jewish, Christian, Muslim Encounter* (Macmillan, 1989). Learned members of three faiths responding to one another on central matters of faith and belief.

Eugene Hillman, *Many Paths. A Catholic Approach to Religious Pluralism* (Orbis, 1989). Extending Vatican II's approach along the lines of Rahner. Good discussions of grace, evangelization and dialogue.

Inter Faith Network, *Statement on Inter-Religious Relations in Britain* (Inter Faith Network, 1991).

Hans Küng (and others), *Christianity and the World Religions. Paths of Dialogue with Islam, Hinduism and Buddhism* (Collins, 1987). Detailed Christian (liberal Catholic) response to aspects of three religions, drawing out common ground and differences. A model of dialogue and full of insight.

Hans Küng, *Global Responsibility. In Search of a New World Ethic* (SCM Press, 1990). Sets out a new imperative for dialogue around the theme: 'No survival without world ethic. No world peace without peace between the religions. No peace between the religions without dialogue between the religions.'

Jews, Christians and Muslims, the Way of Dialogue (Appendix 6 to *The Truth Shall Make You Free: The Lambeth Conference 1988*).

David Lochhead, *The Dialogical Imperative. A Christian Reflection on Interfaith Encounter* (SCM, 1988). Arguing for a typology of Christian responses to world pluralism based on ideological categories, and showing the deficiency of usual classifications. Shows from a Barthian emphasis on revelation how mission is not in opposition to dialogue, but requires it.

Michael Nazir-Ali, *Frontiers in Muslim-Christian Encounter* (Regnum, 1989).

Michael Nazir-Ali, *From Everywhere to Everywhere* (Collins, 1990). Includes a chapter on 'Mission as Dialogue'.

Lesslie Newbigin, *The Gospel in a Pluralist Society* (SPCK, 1989). Calls into question many prevailing assumptions of Western culture, particularly privatised religion and relativist views of truth, and argues for Christ's uniqueness without arrogance towards other religions.

Glyn Richard, *Towards a Theology of Religions* (Routledge, 1989). Further exploration of the theological response to religious pluralism, using major writers in the field.

Vinay Samuel and Chris Sugden (eds), *Proclaiming Christ in Christ's Way* (Regnum, 1989). Contains the Stuttgart Statement on Evangelism produced by evangelicals in the ecumenical movement.

Vinay Samuel and Chris Sugden (eds), *AD 2000 and Beyond – A Mission Agenda*. Includes several relevant articles of high quality.

Ninian Smart & Steven Konstantine, *Christian Systematic Theology in a World Context* (Marshall Pickering, 1991). Trinitarian response from a combined Anglican and Orthodox perspective to a new world setting for doing theology, incorporating insights from non-Christian cultures and religions.

L. Swidler (ed.), *Toward a Universal Theology of Religion* (Orbis, 1987). Presentation of four different Christian views, though all pushing towards universalism, with responses from other religions.

Leonard Swidler, John B Cobb Jr., Paul Knitter and Monica Hellwig, *Death or Dialogue. From the Age of Monologue to the Age of Dialogue* (SCM Press, 1990). Excellent model of dialogue between different Christian practitioners and theologians of dialogue, bringing out the issues of presuppositions and expectations of dialogue in relation to committed faith.

M. M. Thomas, *Risking Christ for Christ's Sake. Towards an ecumenical theology of pluralism* (WCC, 1987). Examining the issues of living in a pluralistic world, with the WCC and India particularly in view, and retaining the ultimacy of Christ.

Keith Ward, *Images of Eternity. Concepts of God in five Religious Traditions* (DLT, 1987). Investigating the supreme reality in the writings of five classical theological figures and uncovering a structural similarity around the theme of the 'iconic vision'.

Andrew Wingate, *Encounter in the Spirit. Muslim-Christian Meetings in Birmingham* (Risk Series, No. 39, WCC, 1988). Describes from the author's experience how dialogue actually takes place, and what results when it happens.

Christopher Wright, *What's so unique about Jesus?* (MARC Europe, 1990). Argues for the uniqueness of Christ together with respect for other religions.

E Publications of the Committee for Relations with People of Other Faiths since 1986

Roger Hooker, *What is Idolatry?* (CRPOF; BCC, 1986).

Educational Principles in Religious Education (CRPOF; BCC, 1986).

John Sargant and Elaine Sugden, *Unfamiliar Journey: Christians and Interfaith Relations* (CRPOF; BCC, 1988). An ecumenical study-guide for use by groups of up to 12 people meeting for 5 or 6 sessions.

Worship in Education (CRPOF; BCC, 1989). Interprets and explains the religious education and school worship clauses of the 1988 Education Act.

Clinton Bennett & Christopher Lamb, *Entertaining Angels* (CRPOF; BCC, 1990). On being hospitable to overseas students, with a useful section on do's and don'ts in approaching those of other faiths in Britain.

Clinton Bennett (ed.), *Invitation to Dialogue* (CRPOF; BCC, 1990). Short essays intended to whet readers' appetites for dialogue.

Roger Hooker and John Sargant (eds), *Belonging to Britain: Christian Perspectives on Religion and Identity in a Plural Society* (CRPOF; BCC, 1991). Substantial essays exploring nationhood and nationality.

Christian Identity, Witness and Interfaith Dialogue: A Discussion Document for the Decade of Evangelism/Evangelization (CRPOF; CCBI, 1991).

In Good Faith. The Four Principles of Interfaith Dialogue (CRPOF; CCBI, 1992). Replaces the earlier *Relations with People of Other Faiths. Guidelines for Dialogue in Britain.*

Discernment, subtitled *A Christian Journal of Inter-Religious Encounter,* is produced three times each year. It aims to provide a vehicle for Christians to reflect theologically on their practical experiences of dialogue here in Britain. It is available from the Committee for Relations with People of Other Faiths, Inter-Church House, 35-41 Lower Marsh, London SE1 7RL, Tel: 071-620 4444, at £6 per annum.